Rainy Day Kids

Ryan Q. Milling

All Rights Reserved, Ryan Q. Milling

The author reserves all the rights to this book. The author permits no one to reproduce or transmit any part of this book through any means or form be it electronic or mechanical. No one may store the information herein in a retrieval system, or to photocopy, record copies, scan parts, etc., without the proper permission of the publisher or author.

RyanMillingBooks.com

Copyright © Ryan Milling 2018

Dedication

I dedicate this book to my family for their unwavering support and most of all, to my mother.

My deepest gratitude to all of the educators that I've worked with.

Rain, rain, go away
    Come again another day
        Me and my friends want to play
    Rain, go away

The rain has so many purposes. The rain gives you fresh water, cools the summer heat, and helps crops grow.

We grew wheat, tobacco, oats, cotton, and sugarcane. We used wheat for grits, tobacco and cotton for the market, and sugarcane for syrup.

Some farmers grow cotton for clothing, while some raise chickens for eggs, some cows for milk, and some peanuts for oil. Others grow hay, soybeans, grain, corn, and peaches. Each is grown and harvested in its own season on the farm.

Farm life can be hard. Sometimes, we had to move to different farms. At other times, we didn't have enough. But Mama always made things fun and made us feel like everything would be alright. It always was.

I guess you can call those cloudy days. On days like these, Mama would tell us jokes and stories. The stories would always help the time go by. Mama would always tell us great things. At least, that's what she used to say.

You see, farmers count on the rainy season. I don't know why, but mama loved to see it rain too.

We would pray for rain. On rainy days, we would get to go to school. Mama always said that learning is something that can't nobody take from you. She would kiss us and tell us to have a good day at school.

When school was over I was always ready to make it home and tell Mama about my day. I would tell her what I learned, and she would tell me more great things. If I liked something she would say, I would write it down and put it in my purse.

School wasn't always so easy. You see, everyone didn't grow up on a farm. They went to school every day. They called us Rainy Day kids because we would surely go to school when it rained.

But I loved school. I dreamed of becoming an orator, pilot, teacher, or secretary. Mama would say,

"Don't drop the dream."

One day while Mr. Heatley was teaching us a math lesson, I struggled and struggled to figure out the problems. I tried my best during class, during lunch, and during recess. When I got my paper back, it had "F" for the grade.

I ran home as fast as I could. I told Mama I hated school, math, and that mean Mr. Heatley. I told her I can't do math. My mama looked at me, took out a piece of paper, and wrote this.

"Can't never could."

I put that in my purse.

At school, I had a really good friend. We even had the same name. Everyone thought we were sisters. I loved her like a sister. She shared, played with me, took up for me, and told me nice things.

My friend Pat and I argued one day. Someone told her a rumor on one of the sunny days. When I returned to school, Pat confronted me about it. I tried to explain to her that I would never talk behind her back and that I knew she didn't like the new boy, named Al, but she wouldn't listen.

That night, while washing dishes, I explained everything to Mama. You know what she told me? Listen now,

"The truth will slow walk a lie down."

I wrote that down and put it in my purse.

I took that lesson and went back to school. Pat and I didn't speak the next day or the day after that. I was so upset with her. I went to her again to explain. The teacher heard us arguing and gave us detention. When I got home and tried to explain, all Mama said was,

"A chain can't rattle by itself."

I put that in my purse too.

Pat and I didn't speak to each other over the next couple of days. I played with other girls and sat by myself at times. When I was alone, I read the various things that Mama would say and that made me feel better no matter the day. Eventually, we solved our differences, and that helped me learn to solve new problems.

During my time at school, Mama would always tell me,

"Never give up on your dreams"

and that

"When life gives you lemons, make lemonade."

I kept all of her sayings in my heart and wrote them down to keep in my purse. On sunny days that we worked on the farm I would read them. I always had a lesson and Mama was always my best teacher.

Sometimes, after it rained, Mama would hum,

"He put a rainbow in the sky."

I remember singing: "Rain rain, rain all day, my siblings and I want to go to school today."

I never quit.

What The Sayings Mean

Don't drop the dream. - Hold on to your dreams and goals and see them through.

Can't never could. - If you think you can't you wont. You will achieve goals when you believe and try to complete them.

The truth will slow walk a lie down. - Untruths can be more interesting than the truth but the truth is steady and will last.

A chain can't rattle by itself. - In order for there to be trouble, both people have to participate.

Never give up on your dreams. - Try and make goals even if others doubt you.

When life gives you lemons, make lemonade. - Make the best out of each situation that comes your way.

www.ingramcontent.com/pod-product-compliance
Lightning Source LLC
Chambersburg PA
CBHW061751290426
44108CB00028B/2954